GREAT BIG WORLD OF COMPUTERS- HISTORY AND EVOLUTION: 5TH GRADE SCIENCE SERIES

BABY PROFESSOR

EDUCATION KIDS

Speedy Publishing LLC
40 E. Main St. #1156
Newark, DE 19711
www.speedypublishing.com

A computer is a general-purpose device that can be programmed to carry out a set of arithmetic or logical operations automatically.

The abacus was initially used for arithmetic tasks. The abacus is the most ancient calculating device known. The abacus is also called a counting frame.

Charles Babbage originated the concept of a programmable computer. His machines were considered as one of the very first mechanical computers ever to be invented. He is considered a "father of the computer".

Early electronic computers, developed around the 1940's, were the size of a large room and consumed huge amounts of electricity.

Colossus was
the world's first
electronic digital
programmable
computer.

Computers as we
know them today
only really started
being made in 1980.

Computers interact
with a number of
different devices
to exchange
information. These
devices include the
keyboard, mouse,
display, hard drive,
printer and more.

Febru
1 2 3 4 5 6 7 8 9 1
16 17 18 19 20 21 22

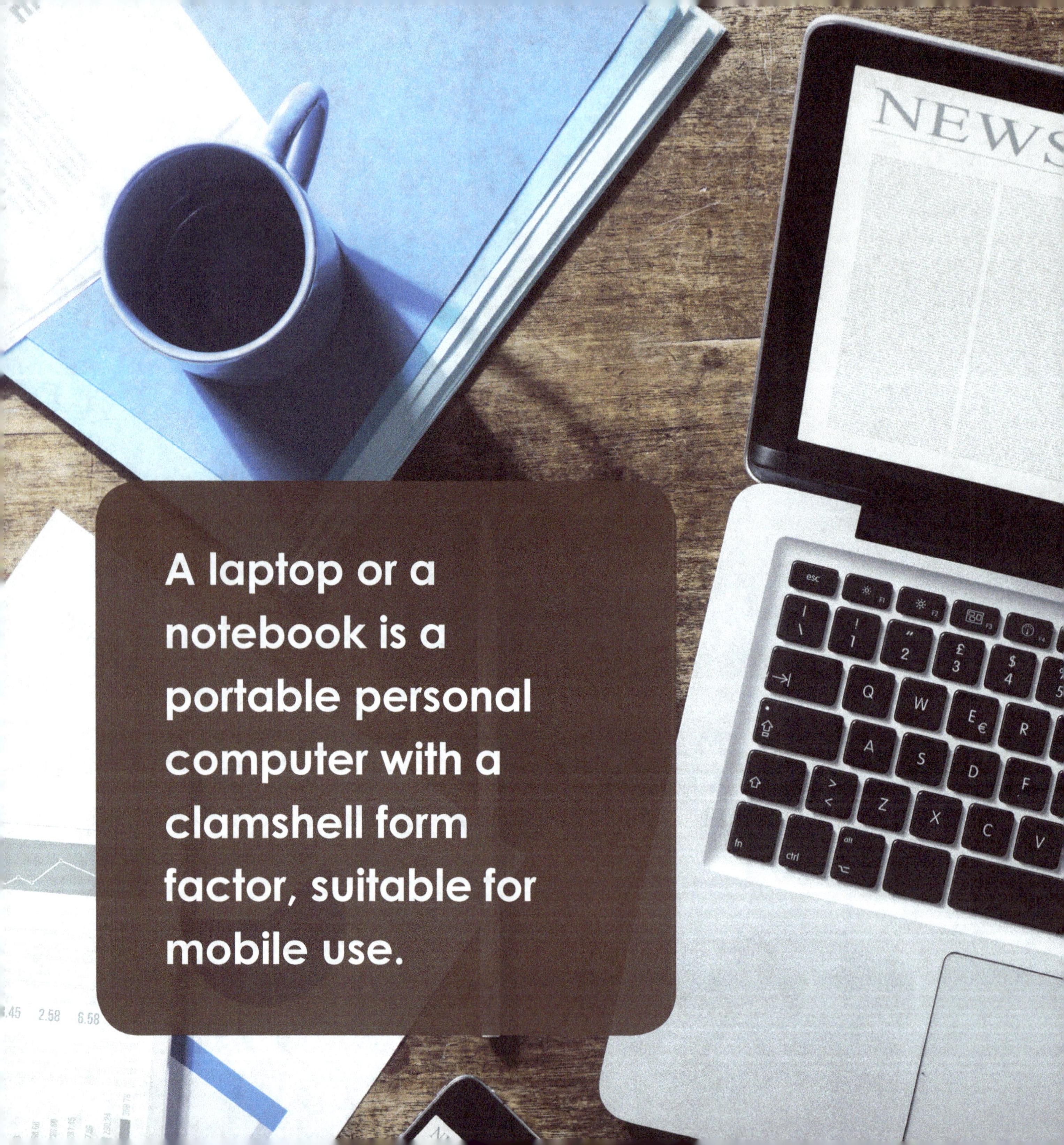

A laptop or a notebook is a portable personal computer with a clamshell form factor, suitable for mobile use.

FINANCIAL REPORT
3.456
2.589
1.258
4.896
3.45   2.58   6.58   12.3
FINANCIAL REPORT
7.42   8.52   6.47
5.42   0.58   6.02
9.42   3.56   7.43

www.ingramcontent.com/pod-product-compliance
Lightning Source LLC
Chambersburg PA
CBHW081244130726
47997CB00009B/2991